MW01196552

"Say Dorothy Allison had a baby with Hans Christian Andersen. That ain't right—I know it, I know—but just say. And say that girl child grows up to wander the tracks, all the while lining up pennies to be smashed on the rails, all the while picking up shed antlers and discarded needles along the berm. And say here comes a fast train, a Christ-haunted train, a train heavy with the freight of West Virginia, a cargo of such great violence and great tenderness that you know the girl is standing far, far too close to all that's barreling past. She stands so close the force of it blows back her hair; she stands so close you're sure she'll get hit and won't survive. But she doesn't step back. No, she stands her ground. This, dear reader, is Sara Wagner, writing this book. These poems ache and ache and ache, but not once do they flinch. Read them and prepare yourself to be wrung out, to be redeemed, to be fit to be tied."

—Nickole Brown, author of *To Those Who Were Our First God*

"Sara Moore Wagner's *Hillbilly Madonna* is a book I have been waiting for. Wagner's family was part of the great diaspora of Appalachian people from the mountains to the cities, and the voice of one raised in that borderland, not quite urban, not quite country, has been long missing from our poetry. No more. And what a voice! *Hillbilly Madonna* offers an unflinching yet tender look at a largely untended girlhood where 'No one told us/how to live as a girl would,/... shave / the holler from our limbs like scraping /paint off an old truck.' These poems are an intoxicating mix of story, myth, image and truthtelling. They compel us 'to really look at it, to see it blinking/through the blackness' – a life, in all its fierce and complicated beauty. Wagner tells us, 'I pick an orange tiger lily with my messy orange fingers, / because I want to remember blooming. / Because I think I could just bloom.' And on these pages, she has."

—Pauletta Hansel, author of *Heartbreak Tree*

"This collection emerges from the intersection of the vernacular world and the empire of divine myth. Father, mother, sister, baby, self—each holds a space in a rough-hewn narrative of abuse, addiction, and survival—and also exists as a looming shadow of its antecedent in the realm of archetype. The canopy over Wagner's creation, and the terrain that buttresses it, is the Appalachian landscape itself, and its synonym, the body. 'When the doctor opens me up, / my bones are gold— / There is some enchantment in them,' she writes. I am wholly enchanted by *Hillbilly Madonna*."

—Diane Seuss, author of *frank: sonnets*

"*Hillbilly Madonna* transports us to West Virginia, into the heart and what it's like to be a sister and a daughter and a mother. Sara Moore Wagner crafts an exquisite balance between beauty and grit in these poems where abuse and addiction loom mythic over the Appalachian panorama. It's such an achievement to craft such a realized world in these poems, ghosts and ache and all. Wagner writes, 'The girls want / water or open skin, that sky, the smoke / of thousands of campfires, sulfur, / the face of a lesser god'—*Hillbilly Madonna* at once confirms and denies these things for them, for us. What an incredible book."

—W. Todd Kaneko, author of *This Is How the Bone Sings*

"In Sara Moore Wagner's poems, girls become women within the beauty and terror of an Appalachian landscape forever changed by the raging opioid epidemic. Wagner's speakers show strength in a world where girlhood is marked by drug abuse, the scriptures, and folk stories passed down through time by fallible mothers and fathers. These poems reach into the reader's heart, leaving a painful yet loving feeling in their wake. They illustrate how interconnected family truly is and how our choices and experiences impact one another in profound and lasting ways: 'I want to ask him how he let himself go so far...and how much of him is left in me. How much will I still need to cut away.' *Hillbilly Madonna* is a haunting and powerful collection and a must read for any poetry lover."

—Erin Carlyle, author of *Magnolia Canopy Otherworld*

HILLBILLY MADONNA
Sara Moore Wagner

INDEPENDENTLY PUBLISHED BY
DRIFTWOOD PRESS

Independently published by Driftwood Press
in the United States of America.

Managing Poetry Editor & Interviewer: Jerrod Schwarz
Poetry Editor: Andrew Hemmert
Cover Image: Caspar David Friedrich
Cover Design: Sally Franckowiak & Jerrod Schwarz
Interior Design: Jerrod Schwarz
Copyeditor: Jerrod Schwarz
Fonts: Cinzel, Merriweather, & Flohart

Copyright © 2022 by Sara Moore Wagner
All Rights Reserved.

No part of this publication
may be reproduced, stored in a retrieval
program, or transmitted, in any form or by
any means (electronic, mechanical,
photographic, recording, etc.), without
the publisher's written permission.

First published November 15th, 2022
ISBN-13: 978-1-949065-22-0

Please visit our website at www.driftwoodpress.com
or email us at editor@driftwoodpress.net.

CONTENTS

III.

"WE CANNOT HAVE ALL THINGS TO PLEASE US,
NO MATTER HOW WE TRY."

GILLIAN WELCH, "ANNABELLE"

Fit to Be Tied

The moon is suddenly there
in the dusty blue sky just like the smooth
flat stones we throw into the pond,
sitting in tall grass, cattails
fat and brown as our legs welted
pink with mosquito bites. Sweat
bees circle your head like a halo;
you blow on a tight reed, taut between
your two thumbs, whistle so loud
the chiggers rise up from the earth
in a cloud. No one told us
how to live as a girl would, to clean
the dirt from our toenails, shave
the holler from our limbs like scraping
paint off an old truck. It's so
hard to tell a star from a lightning
bug when the evening sets; you have
to really look at it, to see it blinking
through the blackness. I lose
your face just like that, the way the bulb
of an insect can go light dark as you trace
it through the sky. Let's play that game
where we lie so still this landscape forgets us,
the crawdads and toads bloom
into the night, until our bodies become
more than vessels carrying in the next
dawn, and the next, until we are this
valley, budding and brilliant hill-scapes,
established and settling stones,
until our father comes shouting,
headlights blazing down the dirt alley,

lifts us into the truck bed, the indentations
smoothing out the outline of the land
from our backs. *One day we will be mothers,*
I say, as the sky races above us and we bump
back and forth into the next stage
of our lives. Summer, even now, gone.

Passing it On

I want to make a child from the one I have lost,
to make the base of her noble by some means, alchemy

the tin girl my father built from junkyard scraps: golden
now. I'll pull her out of my pocket, hunched

in the woods over a patch of clover, show her
to my daughter, say "aren't I so lucky

to keep carrying this with me." Look what I have done
for myself, how far I have come. Bury her deep

in the creeping water primrose roots that strangle
the section of the pond where we search for snails

one after the other, turning them upside down to find a body:
it's funny what's lost, how we pull up fistfuls of empty

spiral shells, how I put the girl I have made deep
into the webbing of organic matter, say live or at least

absorb the heat from the August sky, the tilt of the moon,
Neptune to blue your eyes. It never has worked that way.

Instead, the metal of the girl I let die leaches into the water
supply. We drink it and swell with the grief of being born

like this, swell our fingers, our kidneys and toes, grow
so large the world won't miss us. How we burst open,

vermillion the bank of this quiet space we've tried to sacred,
how we are just one little color now: red. Better for it.

Pre-Heroin

My sister and I follow the wood planks of the railroad tracks downtown. We bought a box of crimson Manic Panic, split two ways, bright red like Tori Amos; shirts tied up, tan bellies. It's a scorcher. the woods mirage. Dirt beneath sweat, unrinsed dye rivulets our faces. I say how much this means to me, to be here with her, walking this path alone to the fair, where I won't have any money but I'll bat my done-up eyelashes at boys until they buy me all the different colors of licorice and enough tickets to ride the Ferris wheel with each one, my backseat sticking to the vinyl.

Every boy has wet hands that soak the baby hairs on my thigh. I'm sunburnt. It hurts to be touched, but I keep going, around and around until night comes and they turn on all those green lights. The rides look like their own city: incandescent. I could be under the sea or on the moon—full of sugar and sun—The breeze just feels so good. My sister doesn't want to ever go home. *No one is looking for us yet. It ain't time.*

We squeeze into a little photobooth with the last of our change. Later, I think that picture was so beautiful, how everything matched then, our sweaty white tees, red faces, splotchy orange-ing hair. How much power we had that night. Just enough to be taken away.

Heroin Ghazal

Growth has lifted the county that buried sunflower seeds
deep into the flesh of every body, buried, sprouting seeds

uncurling green as a smile, and if you do that with enough
bodies, the ground will begin to part in plaits, seeds

expanding into blossoms, petaled heads pointing up
towards a light, until even that light is propagating, it seeds

out over the town, over the small church with its graying
painted windows, an image from Matthew of the sower and his seeds

upon the rocks, and wasn't this such a barren ground before
we started planting deep within gunshot wounds, death now seedy

yellow heads pointed always towards God. We will force this God
into the least of these, the ones who wouldn't grow without seed

on a finger poked into the muscle, just so, placed so shallow, the body
disappears—

Girlhood Landscape

My sister and I buy neon orange fingernail polish
and candy cigarettes. We steal strawberry
jam packets from the diner and sit by the railroad
tracks, painting our nails and sucking out jam. We are all
glossy. We jump from plank to plank with a stick
of candy between our fingers, smoking and skipping
over the boards like stones in a wide river. I tease
her hair up just like Reba McEntire. *You look so good,*
I say. The sky is a corset. It holds us
like breath. We put our last pennies on the rails
when we hear the train whistle miles down.
We jump back, stand just where the conductor can see us
hips out. *One day a boy will reach out of that train,* I say,
lift us up into the caboose like packages and think
of all the candy, the daylight, the lipgloss, the grape
pop, think of all that fun. But she doesn't want to,
her hand in mine, she says *what I want is to be here*
with you. On the way home,
I pick an orange tiger lily with my messy orange fingers,
because I want to remember blooming.
Because I think I could just bloom.

Girl as a Deer Shedding the Velvet

I was born with bulbs
protruding from my scalp,
soft and pliable. These were my ideas
in the strictest sense, new
and warm to the touch.
My first friend was a small
tree, was a railroad spike,
was the knife my father took
to the base of every single thing
I wanted to keep, my body,
my childhood: Uprooted. I was
uprooted. And when I came
of age, all this soft
down, this soft
tore open, petaled
off piece by piece, the red
of me so sharp
and so bright, white
bone—Here I am, still
peeling, almost hard
headed and ready
to hang.

Pending Changes

The woman who gives birth
in the Burger King bathroom, a ball
of heroin on the floor next to her,
sees her infant floating face up
in the toilet, just like the white rat
she flushed as a child over and over,
then days later here it came, wriggling
up, peeping over red-eyed when she played
in the tub. Now on her knees she's
nodding off, watches this baby
she carried like a tumor kick his legs
just how he would kick her ribs,
just how she would kick at the water
to find the bottom or a more firmly
planted stone. The man she came with
is parked outside, slumped over the wheel.
They both saw her growth, the belly
expansion, as a sort of gift, would lie
in the field watching the airplanes
and all that corn, would imagine
themselves being born, the rough
hands of their fathers—the way, sometimes,
being high is the cleanest, softest
bed, how it takes you out, how you might
not even notice the way your body shivers
out the placenta, a round red planet
on the shit-smeared tile. When the cops come,
she is so sure the baby is gone, has watched
his little eyes close over and over, has never
thought to bring him out of the bowl, into
the stinking world. But they find the breath,
there is still breath left, and they are both
pulled out of it.

Deadbeat

Our father goes into the forest and loses
himself, climbs the nearest tree when
night finds him too tired to carry on.
Our father climbs the tree
because he is afraid
of the earth, and me
with this face like wilds.
Don't feed him when he comes
shaky to your doorstep, pleads
to sleep in a corner. He wants
to destroy your house
as if it were a body, as if it were
my body. Wants to tear
you from your sheets with his
teeth, crusts that we
both are. Sister, you are so
fair, the palms of your hands
like new stones. You wreak
axes. Cut him back
to where he came from,
leave him just
as he left us, lost
and trembling—Father,
moon, planet. Our father
who art these things,
our father, an outstretched hand,
a bone hand:
chop it down.

How Could She Have Known

The woman under the sugar maple
looks up at the panicle of blossoms.
They fork out like a child's hand,
open mouthed in a gasp, one falls onto
her tongue, is swallowed. In the night
her stomach grows and inside it
is my mother. Inside it is grief
greater than the length of the roof,
than the wide breadth of branches,
the winged seeds, the eaves which sag
more with each season, weighed down
with heavy little icicles. It's nearing winter
suddenly, seasons corkscrew through
the bark. It's time to bear down
on a hospital bed, to touch
a hand to the hair of a girl so like
fine grass, foliage, a summer baby, sweet
and ready to pour out. And the father says
what is this, how I wish you'd given birth
to a great boar, tusks shrieking through
the West Virginia autumn, impaling
the winter, staking a claim. What is this
blossom, this bud of a girl who's marked
for loss. This mother who's ripe
for chopping.

What My Mother Saw

Just as somehow West Virginia looks different
over the Ohio line on that angular
bridge jutting out of the earth like a fingernail,
on the morning of her mother's death,
my mother looked into her mirrored headboard,
into the shiny brass doorknobs, into the black irises
on her sisters' faces and saw herself
bright and turning as a spindle. She was so
blue eyed, all the boys would call her *bluebell,*
little blue heron, moon jellyfish, the way she'd
move through the hallways, tall. On the morning
my mother watched her mother get shot
in the head, she didn't feel like a jellyfish;
she was 13 and knew every bone in her ribcage,
how fragile the skull, like the bits of hardened clay
in the yard, how your mother can break before
you, even before you break her yourself.

Gross Negligence

Grandfather, in all your greening
silence you'll never recognize
the congress of goslings asleep
in your own house. Never slog
the long road down to your wife,
coil around her, keep her out
of the line of fire, never hold
a towel to the bullet wound in her
head to stave off necrosis, never
take your daughters into your
egoless arms, never cosign on a loan,
not ever. Grandfather, what did you leave
and how stoutly in your own luring,
ireless, energic, full of ice. What
did you sling over your shoulder,
opening the door to the rest
of the wide world, leaving all
those open mouths, coring
out the center of an apple
as you went. Gingerly.

American Anesthetic

You should keep your pain
close as your first bible, write
in the margins of it.
Pain is weakness
leaving the body,
is also a consequence
of life as a woman,
of the apple, of curiosity.
Why wait for a man to come
out of the stained-glass wall, Saint
Bringer of Relief, morphine god, cloth
in hand, to cover your mouth until
you get what he's selling: relief.
Imagine a world where you don't have to
feel it. Clawing and gnashing ceased
by a slow drip needle—and it's like
you are in the world, but not
in the world. You watch your baby being
pulled out one-handed, and you are laughing.
The men from pharmaceuticals come in and yes,
yes, yes you. The room has a pulse so much
like your own, you forget you are dying
for once in your little life. That need:
to forget you are dying for once.

Narcan Metamorphosis

The first time they bring my sister back,
her blood has clotted into a slug.

It creeps through her veins, observes
with its baleful eye the canyons of her, her dark

cornered scissor ribs, how they pierce through
her stomach like a baby's foot,

how the clot finds its way to intestines
where it breaks apart, waterfalls the GI tract

until the doctors have to take that, large and small
intestines replaced with the winding road

we would walk to our father's, up and down
the hill, around the bend.

And again, they take her face, which is the stamen
of a daisy, anther and filament neck, her hair

falling out in clumps, petals. They take her fingers
which shiver notes on the clean white sheets, her toes,

blackened and swollen, her teeth.
The next time they bring her back,

half her heart has turned stone, as if she
has seen her own image in a mirror,

as if she's caved off parts. The doctors go in
with a chisel plow, break up the hardpan soil

between organ and bedrock, remove and replace it
with a bovine valve: cow heart, sister,

and because the cattle are so like us, grieve
when separated, isolated, notice threats and stigma,

branded with stigmata or a name across the side,
she is the same girl, and she returns to the needle again.

Fallout

The reality, of course
is that the sun
is sometimes a mirage
in the sky, that it's still night,
still dark even
if your father says *look out*
the window: sun's rising
like yeast-bread, up and up.
It will look like it's coming
from a different angle, more
northeast, now southeast
and you'll think, *my god,*
we are shifting, must have
been hit hard enough
to tilt. And aren't we all
still lying in our nightdresses,
under the weight of these
bodies—The reality
is that we press our faces
against the glass and look
for light, count on something
that shimmers in
the distance, then fades.
It's not time to wake up, and even
if it were, why
would you want to.

This is Where the Irritation Starts

A dirt road up the side of the mountain:
we cower in the back
of a rickety truck. Our father says,
Look at the trees, look at the trees, look
at the—Years later, he will ask us
to remember what he did for us then
and this will feel like a possum or chipmunk
lodged inside the clavicle. Chest. Daddy,
I tell you I forget everything
because sometimes I am trying
to put a blanket there. Trying to
put a blanket
there, trying. This is where
one sister falls asleep
and the other thinks she is dead,
where the road bumps them
into each other. Where the dead sister
remembers. Where the brother
looks into the wide face of the mountain
and each tree bends to meet
him. The girls want
water or open skin, that sky, the smoke
of thousands of campfires, sulfur,
the face of a lesser god. A lesser
god. Something less.

The First Time

When I lost the baby, the man said   *sleep,*
  and he was above me holding
her body,   a cloud in the sky,
the slow morphine drip   pat, pat.
Time moves in the hallways and firmament,
and I believe it   when the man tells me
about tissue growth on the outside of my uterus.
I am a house being coated in sugar,
over
and over,   my unlit street stretches out
into a path in the woods,   my baby
walks towards me with her hands   up—

I might push her in the oven to have a taste of what it feels like
to be her, walking so young towards empty.

Give me a way or a pill to make this neater,
give me a knife or a needle: another
scene.

Sometimes the Right Light

All of a sudden, sister,
I know what you are holding in—
let go of it. I want to keep
walking next to you.
In the dim evening, scattering
clouds race the semis above us
on the highway; do you remember
walking this road home before, thirsty,
remember stopping at the creek, the moss
like a body, a dead body—
tell me that story again, only
leave out the part where
I wouldn't stop talking and you left
me alone in the tunnel, the great
stones, each one, a grandfather
turtle, beak open—this violence, a routine
crossing—creek bed lit up, second
floor windows yellowing the water.
I am a shadow on the landscape,
invasive. I want you to take me up
in the glass you dip in, catch me
unaware.

Purity Test

One day the world will ask
you to walk through the bees
to see if you are ready or clean
enough to serve, girls
that you are, in all white down
an aisle with the buzz around
or inside you. And maybe like
me you'll want to lay down
in the soil: lion, well fed,
let the bees hive your torso—
consider the wax, the candle,
the flame—how holy it is, how
important, as pure
as the honeybee,
virginal drone—like the work
of Our Lady, heavenly
Mother, blessed with split,
and implantation of our Lord,
with quiet furnish. Consider the wick
of the candle, how it rests inside
the body, how it's lit and destroys
everything. You will build it just
so they can wear it down.

Captivity Narrative

In the middle of the day, the vultures crown
the lake above where you lie
on the shoreline, your skirt knit full
of sugar ants, the sweet of your skin
seeping into the dry clover.
You could almost be the old cow
our grandfather pushed
into the creek bed, released
like a bluegill. Found later, split
open, ribs like fingers. And didn't you know
you were this—unidentifiable
figure, redolent as meat, pickled
in your own age, the salt of every
meal expelled into droplets.
It's the season for it, though,
for lying still in a meadow
while the clouds and birds festoon
the sky, so that anyone could just
imagine it being made for—made in
the image of—where there might
be a pasture beyond this, full
of honeysuckle, where nothing tracks
your slow progress into sleep, nothing
scurries over your arms so small
and dark—invisible world now
suddenly open as a mouth or palm.
Here you are: almost to the molar.
Ripe. Isn't the land supposed to be
here for you, to carry you home
as your feet do your body, little
by little: Plodding and smacking

across every stone until: Doorway
or something else, it never matters
how you get out, only that you
always do.

"ONE MAN'S STORY IS ANOTHER MAN'S SHAME."

WILLIAM ELLIOT WHITMORE
"ONE MAN'S SHAME"

Heroin as Women's Work
after Arachne

This is my first tool: a needle,
chiseled from bone, split headed
as Zeus. I work it back
and forth, stitch through
the tapestry, draw the thread
I brushed, then spun, choke
the wool in my fair hands.
Watch me weave. I'll make it soft
as the rest of the world.
I've built it with this sharp
little point, cinched together
the vast net we drop into the
pond. I feed him even
with this quiet movement,
back and forth. Today, I make
something beautiful. I give him little bits,
first my sleep—take the smooth silk
of my eyes, the yellow of my hair.
Wine-dark work, this. Toil. Fold
my garment around the bones
of every window, black out
the corners. I want to lose
myself in this, to tangle.
Bring me a beam
to tie these threads, a reed
to strike it down, labor light,
the blush of these cheeks.
Bring me someone to beat,
like God, or at least

to see what I've made
of it all. And on my tapestry
I'll show you what I've learned
about God: That a man will take you
no matter how beautiful
you make the world.
No matter how beautiful you make it.

A Waking Image, as Gretel

The rain spills in on us as we sleep
in the backyard, tented. Our brother wakes
with a face cotton-soft, button-eyed, cuts
into us as our grandmother
does the most bruised tomatoes.
Says *run*, but we wait:
sloshing, mermaiding, our hair
and the flowers, the candy
wrappers flood into the yard,
vine. When our father opens
the trailer door he is naked,
his eyes rusted, and we are drenched.
When our father opens
the door he is naked
and will not let us in:
A heavy sigh from the heavy
bed. An uneasy dryness like light.
I remember emptiness, the look of skin,
and so much pillowing rain. My sister, still
a face: The only.

Petrified Figure after CPS X

Our father gifts the world his secrets:
Watch how he takes so much
care with our brother he tears him open at the throat,
butchers him like a deer in the front room,
head to the tile, knife starting
at the groin, blade up, he stops at
each rib, loosens the joints
until pop, and release—brother, naked
and organs before us—our father
is Tantalus, has served this boy now,
skinned and deboned. This is what
a man looks like, stripped of all his better
judgment: A boy is a father's experiment
and lineage, dressed just so.

Witch's Mark

After I stop
shaking, you might find me
filled with holes,
my wrists, punctured
cans, the palms
of my hands: I've been pulled
out of the brambles, pierced.
Maybe you'll want to know how
like a mouth this body,
how the soles of my feet
carry me despite
the missing parts, how the blood
puddles, and yet—my father
is the kind of man, like God,
who would give me to the world
damaged and open,
perforated as a page, flapping
in the wind. When I stop
shaking, when you let me
sit next to the fire, next
to you, you'll want
to ask me how. I'll only say
the word *rupture*; my skin
is this blank page I fill
with batting, wound
after wound
after wound.

Masculine Epidemic

It's like the world slows to a stop when you're high, a plummet into the water at the quarry could be a movie montage: there is the boy, brother: bullheaded poppy in the field, falling heavy and red to the earth from a taut stem. That stem connecting him to his childhood and our father, full of whiskey, to our father's arms. Before he hits, he sends his cry into the stones around him, imagines they hold these last words, the last breath, the man he never wanted to be, the girl he saw running and wanted to catch and tie, the last bite of bread he took, fresh baked, the heat from the oven how it called him to enter and walk through like Shadrach, unscathed as the Christ. In the myth of the falling man, the man does not always die. Because a man is not a man until his father says he is, our brother will climb the tallest face of the quarry, dive naked, nostril full of brown sugar heroin, smack the ice below like a mosquito against a windshield, will feel like Icarus, mid-flight. Will not think of our mother, just how the clouds cradle him, finally held, warm as this winter is, how close that sun.

Legend Says

Our first ghost came from the old railway tunnel, tall as poke-weed she'd glide and sing the songs our mothers sang, ballads like "Swing and Turn Jubilee." *It's all out on the old railroad, all out on the sea.* Sing and sew the road like a spider. She'd weave back and forth over the tracks until it was like the wind took them or the rain, and we'd stand in the tunnel just to hear her or smell her perfume, like White Diamonds, musk and of another time. Stand at the wide mouth of the tunnel to feel her threads around us. In the glint of sunset, at just that time, we'd swear we could see her outlined in all that thread and dust, a web of her in the canopy of oak and walnut. We'd paint her in the tunnel with clay from the creek, and then spray paint her tall or shorter, naked or corseted, we'd make up different stories of how she died. Maybe she jumped and swung from the top of the tunnel, or she wandered drunk out of her mind onto the track when the train was still going. Maybe her husband worked the mine and also never came out, you can see him wandering too, on some nights lantern in hand calling *Mary, Mary, Mary.* If we hide in the rotting trestle, we can see them both some nights call us into the water black as coal. We keep going into the water. Watch us fall over and over: fall and disappear, fall and fade.

Blood from a Turnip

My father's lungs are full
of fungus, great balls of fungus
fibers. Blood clots in the sinuses.
The doctors go in with knives up, masks:
Tear them out by the roots,
or carve away at him piece by piece.
He calls to say *I still can't breath*—
coughs up so much blood
the plywood walls collapse,
the dividers, the hospital.
We are out in the yard
with the wild turkey he raised
from chick. I want to hold
the waste of his breath,
the round mucus gobs
in my hands to show him
I know how to care
for something, too—I know
how to take care of myself
better than this. I want to ask
him how he let himself get so far
gone that the mold grows even
on his insides. And how much
is inside me, then—how much
of him is left in me. How much
will I still need to cut away.

Autoimmune Anemia: Transfusion

When I thought you were going to die
I planted a hosta in our yard, next
to the pond you built for the bluegill
you caught, the one so small it looked
like a goldfish, but you knew what it
was even though. Even though.
And there is that fence you built to keep
out the ally trash, and the neighbors.
And it's so tall. When I thought you were
going to die, I asked you to dance with me
and you said you can't, but I keep seeing you
move out of the corner of my eye, and you
are like a ribbon of cloud I want to cultivate
and bind, to bury. To be a daughter who tends.
To have a father who wants
tending or burial. For you to be that father
or little root in the dry earth. But you are still so
yellow, your face, your image a dying
lemon. And I want to tell you I will come to you
as a fully-grown catfish, and I will eat all
the dirt you've piled into this. And it will be
alright. It will.

Farther that wasn't there
but now is then

Because God Demands Silence

Remember that time you watched me
curtsy to the devil just so, tilting my heel
up as if stepping off the stoop
at grandma's house, all light
and full of wind. You knew what I was doing.
The canary came then, dug its beak
right between my fingers, made me a mother
before I was ready, pulled out all the milk
and worms from my skin. Wasn't I beastly,
my hair rotting leaves. Yes, I know the scriptures,
how Isaiah calls me to be a royal diadem
in your hand, inscribed in the palms
of your hands, but didn't the devil
offer to feed me a ripe apple
cobbler fresh from the oven, mounds
on mounds of cherries if I'd only open
my mouth. When you were born, I was already hard
featured, ill-fated. Already so starving
for language, I called the birds
to me, goldfinch, cardinal, carried
them on my knuckles like jewels.
I keep walking open mouthed around the yard.
Feed me. I perch in the rafters, walk
toe to heel, arms akimbo. I gussy
up my skirt so high you start to see
what I mean by wanting something else,
how this body needs something more to do.

Jack and Jill

Remember
when I rolled
downhill at church
camp, until even
my belief undid
like my ponytail,
the way the clothes, the threads
unraveled and spun back
onto the spool, and my mother
unpricked her finger, unthreading
the needle, it all moving
backwards and gliding. And then
I never wore that dress he liked
so much, never sprained
a thing, never bashed
against a rock, rock
of ages. I am ten
and I hold a piece
of wafer in my chest, sweet
wine seeps from my knee, gravelly
and hot, sweat bees circle
like a crown—I am undone
as a zipper,
and I notice what's left
of my body, feel
with my hands, soft
against each arm. I'm ok
still, girl still, between
my legs a gust
and shadow grows.

Birth Story

Thinking more of her baby more than herself

In the hospital, the nurses think
my blood thickens too easy, inside
it clots like pomegranate seeds,
when they hook me up to the IV,
it falls out, clogs the line—jewels—
Thin me out—
they force my womb to contract.
Imagine a fist, a lens tightening—
the Pitocin, a bit of smoke
in a wide cave. Hello, little girl,
come into the light, out
of the thicket, of the thickness,
of me. Learn how to eat, to
suck the marrow
from each of these bones, to use
my body as another kind of house,
the ducts in my breast, tiny rooms
full of sunlight. Draw it all out. I want
to make your first gown
from this thickness, to cover
you, skin to skin, to be
the mother I always wanted, someone
not so aware
of bleeding.

hopefull and evning mom

Protective Services

Nights I lay like arms
across a torso, the way
my nerves look, smallness
of veins. Like tributaries,
the world spawns as the catfish
do in the lake. The raw center
where I drown and re-drown
my father, then the image
of this new child.

Remember Hecuba,
her 19 babies, how she was
also born from a river-
god. Some days I want
to drill my hand to the headboard.
To keep dreaming
I sent my own self away,
mouth full of cotton.

Instead, I hold a hot spoon
to my eye until I am half
blind as Cassandra, until
I forget my mother's
bruised arms, the bends
of them empty as a syringe.
How if they let us, we both
could spread into the ground
system, fork like lightning in the earth.

Girlhood Schism

My daddy runs me
in his dune buggy up the hill
and right down into the holler,
into mess, until water
and muck fleck across my face
in the shape of a hand. I am
corrected for what I have been:
clean and girly, hands folded
under me like my mother taught,
if you don't know what to do,
just sit on your hands, keep
them down. Everything here is damp,
vegetable green, musty like rot, full
of organic matter. I want
to be inside my little room
bashing Barbies together
like gongs, calling my
adulthood in with plastic
movement, so precise.
In the buggy, I fold my arms
over my face and wait
for stinging dirt needles,
whipping branches to stop
shredding me like barbecue pork.
I don't know what I am, want to be
unseeded, un-fathered, unseen,
I want to get out of this
piped coffin my father built
from junkyard parts.
Even the smell of rust
on the door frame is foul,

is rancid as we are,
clustered together like this,
teaching each other a lesson.

Parable of the Father as Pinocchio

He is a wooden boy hungry,
finds an egg under a lamppost,
smooth as a cumulous cloud.　　　It's morning.
There are frying pans
on every stove, vegetable oil.
bacon fat brown.
A voice says,　　　*Just crawl in*
through a window.　　　Voice,
then a foot on the ledge,　　　oomph.

Notice the cricket he's smashed
into a tissue inside his little pocket.

Because he never had a mother,
because he needed to find something
to put in his casket of stomach.

Not so much the break-in,　　　but the egg,
full of all the organs
spleen, kidneys, appendix, lungs,
a bladder sweet and full, plopping
out onto the skillet, and　　　o gorgeousness,
　　　o hunger,　　　o now.
O boy with your wooden face turning.

This is what I'll always remember wanting.

On Cutting Him Off

If the rulemaker is my father who ties my hair to the tree
behind my house, who watches the stunned earth
turn, the noodles in the pot boil down to nothing,
who serves me that nothing when I am naked
and most hungry, when I've got both of my hands
over my belly, when I'm hiding that softest part
of myself. If the rulemaker sees me and says spread
your arms like a compass, like a tape measure, let
me see how much you take up, how much space
and air, how many hairs of yours would it take
to weave your own burial wreath, so that nothing
of mine is taken. If the rulemaker is my father
and he is sitting in a hut in the woods, whittling
the last of my bones into a whistle he'll use to call
his best dinner, all those pheasants and crows
from the meadow. *Who will bake your savory
pie, father, who will pluck out the feathers and the eyes?*
If the father is the one who spreads the rules
like butter or seed, who plants them, who feeds
the chickens out back, who carries the eggs, how
can we. What can we. What are we. How can we.
I am already dead here, father. I am already
under your feet. I'm not doing anything but letting
myself be laid rested. If my father has tied me
to the tree by the hair, it's only natural
to cut it off.

Old Wives Tale

What can we understand
of history except this: a figure
walked the wall beside our grandma's
house night and day, day and night,
and if someone took a picture, it must
have happened. An apparition, I think.
Someone was happy or unhappy,
and her hair shown in the wind
like a dove. We thought it was
some kind of bird, but our mother
said *silly, silly*. Later, we pretended
to get married like we saw the girls
do on TV because it meant we'd grown
up enough to let a man tell us
to come in now and sit down,
to let a man grunt his sorrow into
our little ears just when we wanted to stop it. Just
stop it. We pretended to dive
off every bridge in all white, hand fasted.
I said to you, *promise me if we die*
tonight, we'll come back here
looking like this. We'll sing Glory,
Glory, Glory—Almighty.
It'll terrify. I always leave
something out here, misrepresent
the narrative. Walk the wall with me now,
full grown, hen-tied. Invent
a tale with me to replace
the truth of it all. Help me undo
our childhood like an old corset,
the past nothing more than
scratchings at the door
or on the page.

"I OWN EVERY BELL THAT TOLLS ME."

NEKO CASE, "AT LAST"

Forgetting the Dust of Her

Our mother cleans the laundromat in the evenings
for extra money, and I go with her, watch
the tired clothes spin in the big barrel washers,
slicked in foam, whopping the glass like little hands.

A figure forms in the cotton, another girl,
wide hipped, arms out. She, Tide-full, sashays around
in the drum with a pump, pump, pump.

Our mother runs her fingers along the lint traps so fast,
splits gray from vent like a pit from a ripe peach—
so clean. Mother watches me watching.

I get bored, tired of her; I rifle through the old magazines,
Ladies Home Journal or Redbook with the menthol cigarette ads,
recipes for brown butter bourbon cake, Maybelline—
this is what I should be, Cover Girl, cherry sweet—

I start spinning round and round in one of the faux leather
swivel chairs by the window, lose myself in speckled ceiling panels.
My body is a round spindle—I can't see or hear her.

The dots on the ceiling could be stars or galaxies,
the hum of the machines the drone frequency of the birth
of the universe, over and over. I am all foam, now vapor,
and it doesn't matter what's on the other side of the glass.

In the End We are All Daughters

In the story, the mother loves   only the ugly sister,
     so we know the ugly sister must be bad, and the one
who is unloved: a shimmer on the face is a shimmer
     in the soul, and God looks kindly on clean beauty,
a still white landscape,   on her.
The pretty sister must find a real mother,
beneath the water, a Mother Frost, long toothed and ageless,
to love her.   In this story, you will
want to be the pretty sister,   only daughter.
Not the one who is ugly and lazy as a fern,
For beauty, you prick you own fingers:
     let red into every stitch.
Walk yourself back home,   find a new home, all gold,
golden hair, golden child.   Avoid your little pitch one, sticky girl
who gets too tired to work, lays down in the grass,
does not take the bread out   so it burns, does not shake
the apples from the tree.   Let her tend your bed,
punch it down so hard the feathers cover all that tar,
your face: Be made avian, skinny
wrists: carpus. This is how to be the beauty you imagined
when your mother first shuttered you into the world. How you'll remember
you were made from her,
stone from the land, snow   from the sleepy sky.

How to Cope

A long time ago, I built a stick house
by the railroad tracks in the backyard
of my childhood,
covered myself with leaves and the earth
was as small as my bony wrist.
I was escaping
like our father always
has, to the woods.
Later, the sheeted cold,
the sky metallic
as a gun barrel and not one thing
was natural or small, not one thing.
This is the secret: buried
under brush, osage oranges piled
like landmines, no one came
to find me. The mind of a parent
can keep you in your bed, tucked even
when you are lying
under foliage, heavy as your own
body. I don't want you to be afraid to walk
shoeless into the wide field, but look
at how the ground splits beneath us
like a cantaloupe rind dropped,
these seeds—imagine
safety while the girl sleeps
alone, the buzzing of mosquitoes,
the rattle of passing. You'll know
what the world looks like, how
sometimes nothing is watching you
slip away.

Cattleheart

My cow stands in a field
with its white hairs and patches of brown
like a broken sky. Cow
with its brown eyes wet
and so full. It says, *you*

tell me what it means to have skin
and I will tell you what it feels
like to have wide eyes like an animal.

Cow, I found you standing
over the grave
of your mother and lowing.
This was after my father
cut off my hands. You told me
how to live in a world
as a beast would. When I speak now,
it is only lowing.

Stop—Let's imagine this pasture is an ocean.
The clouds are the same, no matter.

My cow bends down its knees
to see if there is a reflection
of this in the grass, but there isn't,
only the rocking of the world
and our solitary, wounded body.

I say, *we are meat* but it is so foreign
it could be the noise of a blue whale.

When we die, someone might notice our grave and stare out into the vastness.

We are That Farmer's Daughters

What does she not feel,
with the inside of her body looking so
planted we can see the bitter marigold
of her thought rise up out of her chest, rooted
and orange. When we go to her this morning
cools. We change our bodies into trowels,
dig her out and split her. Forgive me if I think this
is what anyone should do, focus
on the most essential parts—this morning
and girl with her edible flower blooming.
A potato just under the surface. Let me make
you breakfast in this light, with your face
looking so temporary, too. And you are. Morning
spreads like the thin veil of blood around the brain.
It's important to be here, to keep on.

I Have No Love for Images

I've given up on the idea that a man
can crocus out of the earth all hair,
even his feet covered with hair, out of the earth
like a swollen root, his hands as soft and full
as berries. Because I am not
a tamer, but a shivering vine
and I also come
from this gorged stem, fruit
and not harvester. Forget
me for a second, you have given
up on this man out
of the ground because he is not
Adam but a fleshy bit of death,
and when he does get sick
and naked, when
he throws a bleeding thigh
so near the sun it hots
and smells like meat
our mother boiled down so low
it turned to dust—this thigh he cuts
from a living bull, from your sacred
body—And if you want to know,
I've been searching for him, too.
I want to eat the stone bread
which stands for days, which stands for God,
to not sleep like a snake in a pile
of filth, to feed myself on air and the prettiest
slivers of sky. To be made
an equivalent beauty, or else
to not die is what I mean.

Idle and Lawless

All beautiful like the side of the hill,
dirt and rocks and wildflowers; the mosquitos
low over the rain-filled tire tracks.
Bees hover, test the sugar
in our sweat. With lit cigarettes pressed
between our lips, we flick the ash onto the wet
side of the earth: we are playing boys,
Tom Sawyer and Huckleberry Finn.
The creek is high.
We wade barefoot, jeans rolled up
to our inner thigh, we are looking
for an image to latch onto, to start us rolling
through the rocks. We want to run from something,
towards something, to solve the mystery, to get out.
*I don't want to be Tom, I say, because he always
was clowning and let's be real, I am the smart
one.* Will build a raft from all these sticks,
will leave you with that needle in your arm
like a box of stolen gold. Will leave you because
I can. Am making you this story just
as a blood oath: I will borrow your lines
and flee west. I'm always the one
to run from it. I'm always the one to run.

Heroin as Jack the Giant Killer

When you come into his yard with your long feet,
long nosed, big-breasted, full of holes, he will trap
you like an ant under a glass, aim the sun
in on you until fire. With his other hand,
he'll piece you out like mincemeat pie,
chunks of your thighs into his mouth.

He is the fat friar who sneaks into your bed
at night, curtains drawn.

He'll tell our father he owns nothing,
will take nothing, and you are no girl,
just a body cresting the horizon
like a mountain, so large. Just a mission.
Who would want you like this but him.

Later, he'll wear your head like a top hat,
will trade his old little crown for a rake,
for a plow. Will plow you, plant you, reap
you like grain. Leave you. Will wander
those long prairies alone, so green and sprightly.

So holy. So tame. No one, not anyone will know
another name: Just Jack,
and Jack comes out clean.

Scheduled Induction

Fit under it, as a brick
under laminate, as the unbranched
roots of moss gathering
inside the bathtub. Fit somewhere
inside my torso, curled in like
my intestines. This is what organs
do, but you are not organ, not
organ but girl. In three days
we'll shave away what keeps you
imaginary, strip the cervix, break
the water, and you'll be above the earth
as the single-celled leaves, you'll be
vascular, not really—you'll be skin
and bones, moving on the surface
of my body, all eyes and gums.
Before you are born, I want
to say I am sorry for what collects
in me, and in this house, what you
will have to clear away
to clean yourself, sorry
for each chill and shake,
that we were not both born
simpler, able
to pull up what we need
from the soil, to cover
in shade, to keep fitting
under until we're ready
to come out, alone
and unassisted—

Elements of Decay

On the road up the side of our mountain, through the chinks
in the trees, there's evidence we cared for something,

a decorative awning over a sagging porch, black streaked windows
busted out and boarded, beyond there is a hand carved mantle.

Through the layers of cardboard patching the hole
the water has worn under the sink, there's a foundation

laid by hands ready to call the land home, to cut away
the wilderness and sleep, poison ivy boiling the surface

of the skin like the rusty water in the pot on the wood stove.
Boiling water and skin means work, to be ready to work for a bed

with sheets hung out in the sun. Until the hunger comes,
and we all are on our knees in the church, opening our mouths

for bread. And like those crows who swoop down to steal
even the light, we'd eat the fire blooming on the candles,

the wick, the wax, we'd eat the fingers of the father, eat the
sandstone cliffs, the whisper of a bobcat in the woods.

We are hungry, want to adapt to a landscape claiming
back what we took from it, our bodies sinking into the soil, pulled

down like the siding we keep pushing up with anything we can find
that sticks. And like we do, the trees put their roots

in the creek to cool off, and that, too, looks like shelter.
When we walk the frogs and snakes disappear into it.

Mark on the World

When the doctor opens me up,
my bones are gold—
there is some enchantment in them.
The clock on the wall
rattles and speaks. Says,
put her as you found her,
into the womb of her mother.
When the doctor closes
my skin, my breasts
are two blinking eyes that watch
him move his needle back
and forth like a pendulum.
The bed quakes, the light
is a fiery god—Pantagruel
vomits up the sky.
I am a piece of tooth
in the great mouth of the world.
The dust of my core is
rot. Fix me,
oh you firmly planted
flower of the world.
These vibrating fingers
are my only stems.

Meleager

There is so much fire under the floor here.
God help you if you walk barefoot
or your skin is made of dried leaves.
If your eyes are full of the particular fuel
that lights well on dry nights, like this one—
always turning.

This is the only light
after all. This night.

If you keep picking
grass even after there is no more fire
to light it with, when even the bones
of your house are fleshless,
your blood and your dry tongue puffed out
like a bird.

God help you when you think, this is what ash feels like.
A snuffed-out brand. My mother, you kept me out
of the oven for so long, but still.
Not all life hinges
on fire or brands—
then, perhaps dryness keeps
it going.

Like the World Could Bend and Fall with Us

We saw our fathers go down first,
in the aisle of the old church, in the boards we carried

on our backs to the cleared field. We erected
simple and whitewashed, a single steeple.

We were given the gifts of the spirit, speaking
in tongues or a touch of the healing

we brought from the chapel into the yard
where we'd lay hands on the red earth of each new grave.

Lay hands on each little baby brought year after year
to the front of the church for dedication and blessing.

We sang the holy songs first from hymnals,
then the new projector Pastor would roll over

the orange carpet, wearing a line of gray
straight down the center. How we'd dance

that line, hands in the air, sweat dripping
into our stockings and then into our church shoes,

clang of cymbal and tap on the keys, pat pat of feet.
Only the best of us would meet the lord early,

would be slain in the spirit, prostrated, overcome, anointed
and prone on the floor near the water stain, near

the pocked wood pew, nearer to the adoration of the town,
of the sky. And then, how the spirit moved in us to speak

and speak, to eat the bread, drink the sweet juice decanted
into little plastic cups, to touch hands upon leaving,

remember the Pentecost is the act of the spirit entering
the apostles, what they do with it, how far they go,

down to the floor, restored in front of the congregation,
walking home like something might be different.

Even if These Promises Are True

In the spring the oak trees bud leaves small
as a mouse's ear. All the fathers abandon
their children, wives folded
into torn sheets, to go hunt
morels, tucked close to the bark—
oak, ash, elm, hickory, sweet
naked morning, shoeless and stripped
as the apple orchard. And then why
does the morel love a tree, tied
either to roots or dirt, they grow
and regrow, and our father never
knows enough to tell us why, just
that a fungus, bulbous and blonde
as a daughter, comes back and back
again, each year, triggered by the loss
of winter, a snap of warmer days,
the first promise you've overcome it,
you will overcome it. Wake
to our father hovering over you
with a dish of them, meaty and tender,
sautéed simply in fresh Amish butter,
or battered and fried, stuffed full
of cream cheese, and you will eat
and eat until you feel better,
until you forgive him for it,
for abandoning you to hunt,
for developing his eye to always
turn to the earth, to the dark soil,
to the roots, then body
of the sycamore where if nothing
is budding, at least he can tap it,
drink that water sap, keep on.

Here is the World Father Built

There are no God Winks, no God's eye
in a cardinal. Even though Grandfather
loved cardinals, no shadow. He also loved guns,
would clean the lead deposits in the bore chambers
with peroxide and vinegar. Mama
became a rifle champion after
her mother's murder,
and even though I never saw her do it, I can imagine
her putting her eye to the sight, honing
on the way a bullet explodes on impact, how it mirrors
what the body does, what an apple does
when tossed from a high window. Chunked.
There are pamphlets for cleaning a body,
shipping a body. If you are the one
who lives, gets out by crouching behind a wall
or under a desk, there will be white crosses,
you will have to visit the white crosses, see compact,
smiling faces flash like skulls before you.
Remember John the Baptist, who abandoned his wife, was torn
to pieces and sold; you can visit his head in Rome, right hand
in Rhodes, a tooth in Bulgaria. This is what men do:
A man may leave you for God, or the devil,
for Greece, but you will still want to keep
his putrid heart in your desk, wrapped
in paper and stinking.

Let's Wait to Bathe Her

When the baby comes, sweet
in a layer of vernix, sticky
and white as my first panties,
laid on my chest, folded
mess of skin, I am just this:
a platter of stone, bones
stacked on top of each other.
People say *you can heal*
your childhood through
this child. I take her
into the cabin he abandoned
me in, forest-thick
girl incased in cream,
undressing in whatever
light, a beam of gold a thread—
maybe I can be what she needs,
or else, what I see
when I look in the mirror—
clean.

A Conversation with Sara Moore Wagner & Jerrod Schwarz

Sara, let me start by saying how much of a joy it's been to read and publish this collection of poems! There are a myriad of themes to dive into, but I want to start our discussion with one of the book's major concerns: place. *Hillbilly Madonna* is rooted in Appalachia and does not shy away from the unique traumas of the region. When you were drafting these poems, what felt vital to communicate about this geography? Moreover, are there any aspects of this setting that you feel have been overlooked or misrepresented by others?

Thank you so much, Jerrod! That idea of place was such a fundamental element I considered when writing and compiling this collection. I'm someone whose parents divorced early, so I've always had a foot in two worlds. My mother is from West Virginia, so she is, in some ways, "more" Appalachian than my father, who is from the foothills of Ohio's Appalachia. Both of their families relocated to Columbus, OH when they were in their teens, which is when they met and had me.

When I began this book, I wanted to primarily understand my father's landscape—how deeply rooted in me, which was symbolic. My mother had a desire to separate herself from it. She went to college when I was five and worked about a hundred jobs to help give my younger siblings and me opportunities we wouldn't have had without her. My father wanted every part of "hillbilly" identification in an almost stereotypical way. He made it his identity. He loved camo, bean dumplings, he raised chickens and turkeys in his urban backyard, which was full of scrap metal and old parts. I spent my summers and so much time stomping through the holler and being run through the mud in his "dune buggy." A lot of my father's disappointment in me was that I did want another life. He always felt judged by that. When I went to college in Northern Ohio, people saw me, my slight accent and lack of "polish" as hillbilly, which was a new experience for me. To me, I was, and I was not.

When I was writing these poems, I went back to my childhood physically. I stayed in Jackson, OH and Tar Hollow State Park to really be sure to inject that landscape, to get the images right and be inspired by whatever ghosts of me were still there. It did feel vital to me to establish a setting, mostly because it's so tied to my own identity in so many complicated ways I am still trying to understand.

It was important to me, too, to not speak as if I understand fully or am speaking for the entire community, which is diverse and complex. I think the book *What You Are Getting Wrong About Appalachia* by Elizabeth Catte does a really good job of defining what Appalachia is, both geographically and culturally, in that she really stresses, through essays and in her introduction, that Appalachia is "a flexible regional identity that has nothing to do with ethnicity." It's not all the straight, white, uneducated, coal mining people the media portrays. It's a vast region. I've come to understand myself as an "urban Appalachian," as someone born in another city to Appalachians who migrated for work and better opportunities.

Pauletta Hansel, a poet who came of age in the early days of what can be thought of as an Appalachian Literary Movement, has written about the ways in which embracing Appalachian identity was used both in the region and in Cincinnati to craft a voice against injustice, and to accentuate the positive qualities of an often-maligned people. In this book, that is something I am deeply exploring, but I don't want to oversimplify or imply the region is in any way homogenous. Catte says "Appalachia is nothing if not messily defined." There are people of all economic backgrounds in the town my family comes from. It's important for me to stress, then, that I speak for only my own experience and not for the region as a whole, as so many others in politics and popular media have done. I wanted to not overlook or misrepresent things, being someone who has been transported to this weird suburban life I now live.

Of course, I can't speak about misrepresentation without bringing up JD Vance. Pauletta Hansel, in her essay "My Father, JD Vance, and Me" discusses how she is from the same town as JD Vance's family (Jackson, KY), how he is part of a long history of those who have "othered" Appalachians for specific political agendas, how different she, her father, and the region are from his description. His story is very similar to mine. I even had a therapist, when hearing about my childhood, say "have you read

Hillbilly Elegy?!" Vance is running for Senate, endorsed by Trump. His signs are everywhere in my neighborhood. His entire political career is built on the idea that he got from hillbilly to Yale with a stronger work ethic than the other people in his hometown of Middletown, OH, a town fifteen minutes from where I live now. It's a common perception that poor people, addicts, the unemployed don't want to work or improve their situations. This is the grossest misrepresentation. As Catte says, "Many Appalachians are poor, but their poverty has a deep and coherent history rooted in economic exploitation." Much of what is said about Appalachia continues to exploit this region.

When I think about my own story, I disagree so intensely with the sentiment that people can just "pull themselves up by their bootstraps" with more hard work and elbow grease. I am only here writing about this place and these people because I had specific privileges and people (my mother) who would pull me up out of whatever I got myself into and set me back on the path. The girls I grew up with and family members who fell into addiction and never got out are not "worse" than me. Had I not been put back on the path time and time again, if I didn't BELIEVE there was a better life for me, who knows what person I would be today. It's not about personal fiber, it's about hopelessness, poverty, and systemic problems and pressures that keep people stuck and searching for a way to numb that pain. No one is "better" for making it out, and the more we look that in the face, the more likely we are to enact real change. People need work that pays a living wage and doesn't destroy them, better educational opportunities, public programs, and support—that's where to start.

Your book does a fantastic job of conveying Appalachia as a complex place, and I wanted to know if there are any facets of this geography that did not make it into this collection but that you want to write about in the future. Perhaps more specifically, are there elements of this place that you want to keep exploring in writing?

Yes! Because my family, particularly on my dad's side, has always been poor, a lot of our family documents and genealogy have been lost. This is fascinating to me because, growing up, I was told my grandfather was 100% Native American, a mix of Cherokee and

Seminole, which is a tribe not native to Ohio. In Ohio, Indian removal treaties of the early 1800's dismantled all Native tribes, claiming that land for America. They removed many individuals, but not all. In many cases, they destroyed or falsified documents of those left to the point where people would say "there are no Indians in Ohio."

I have no idea how much of what I understand of my own lineage is true, and how much is family lore. For a long time, I considered that a big part of my identity, but I want to explore what that means, especially within the context of Ohio, a land where every tribe was dismantled. My aunt traced our lineage back as far as she could, finding some documents and things, to a chief named Ernest Big Chief, but a lot of it is still so confusing and fractured.

I have read articles about how the Appalachian Mountains were a haven for displaced people of all kinds, and I think that is the angle I want to explore. There is such a rich history regarding race. But, somehow, the stereotype of an Appalachian is white. Of course, I am also white, so I don't want to claim a culture or identity, but more to understand the place my family comes from, and to maybe dismantle even more of those stereotypes of what an Appalachian is.

As an editor, I've had the duty of reading many poems about parental trauma. *Hillbilly Madonna* is a harrowing render of this trauma that goes beyond the speaker's explicit suffering to investigate generational histories. I'm particularly struck by one poem opening with "Grandfather, in all your greening / silence you'll never recognize / the congress of goslings asleep / in your own house." As a poet, what advantages (and disadvantages) do you have when communicating truths about family?

As poets, we have the gift of not being memoirists. We get to walk that line between invention and truth. The truth, often, can be more important than the facts, particularly when poets are trying to address large topics like generational trauma. You can't tell everything, and you have to hide and reveal certain things for impact (whether it's an image or an event). Some of these things can come out of sequence, can be altered, or can even be invented.

When I write, I can do a burlesque. I can reveal or hide whatever I want to. My responsibility is to the greater truth, and to language and sound, more than to telling every little fact and detail about every person.

That being said, breaking that cycle of trauma was such an important part of the crafting of this book. Like the research I did about place, I actually researched family divorce and arrest documents to try to understand more of what both my parents experienced. My mother's childhood was riddled with violence and abandonment, and my father was a rebel farm-boy whose father was the subject of my first chapbook, *Hooked Through*. His father took his own life. There are also hard things about siblings and friends that I've put into poems here.

I do wrestle with speaking about family because I want to tell my story and also protect people I love. My mom said I can't write about her until after she is dead, so I really try to not over-tell her story, until she is ready. My father passed recently, and he didn't ever read my poems anyway, so it's never really been an issue there. The "tell it slant" aspect is important. If I'm telling a secret, one that might hurt, I'm going to protect that person by changing their relationship to me or by using those poetic devices of metaphor or persona to pillow it. I think the truth is important, but so is family. I've told secrets here, but none you can easily trace to one person.

There's also the disadvantage that, because poets write in metaphor and go beyond the literal so often, a person close to me could see themselves in a poem that is not actually about them. I find I have to explain my work a lot more to family, to help them understand the larger picture. My mother and my husband understand this and support me, even in poems where I'm very critical of mothers and husbands.

Ultimately, I see this as a book about breaking cycles. For better or worse, I needed to show the cycle in order to get the hope of breaking it to come at the end. We are not chained to our tragedies and weakness.

I love the duality in stating, "I think the truth is important, but so is family." Most poets writing in 2022 are influenced by the Confessional Poets and the accompanying push toward an unwavering

revelation of trauma. I can still remember being a nervous undergraduate student and having a professor say, "If you're worried about what your family may think, just don't show them the poem." What advice would you give to new or young poets looking to write about generational / familial issues?

That is so funny, because I remember distinctly giving a reading after undergrad and a fellow student came up to me and said, "I didn't realize you used I so much in your poems" in a way that was so derisive I still think about it. So, I tried to avoid the "confessional" label for longer than I should have. Now, I think I balance just on the cusp of confessional—some poems more than others.

A mentor and friend of mine, the poet Kelly Moffett, told me I was too much in my head without enough heart, and that really convinced me to let more of myself into my poems, research and persona blended with confession.

I know it's a blessing that my mom reads all my poems, but that also means I can never just *not* show her. I also think about my children (I have three). One day they will maybe become interested in these things, maybe even after I am gone when I can't explain what I meant and what is truth vs. what is invention.

So, I guess my advice would be to think about it later. Write what you need to write, but there's always room to shadow in revision, to change a relationship or a name, or a series of events just enough. Like I said, poetry is not memoir. If you're worried about hurting someone, and you can speak the truth without hurting, that's part of the art of it. Of course, the people who hurt you most are generally the ones who don't care or won't read it—and if they did, maybe it's something they needed to hear? I'd say go with your gut. Speak through your silence in whatever way you need to.

But, I do think if you're writing someone else's life story, even in your own family, ask their permission. Some people want to tell their own story, and you'll want to be sure you don't oversimplify, appropriate, or misrepresent someone else's trauma.

Sometimes you might want to call everyone out—I am also on board with that.

One of my favorite aspects of this collection is how it positions womanhood at the center of discussions around the opioid crisis. It's hard not to think about these intimate and focused poems in the context of larger media representation around the epidemic (in the recently released show *Dopesick*, the female lead dies midway through the season, whereas Michael Keaton's character recovers and gets his medical license back). What advice would you give to other poets and writers looking to speak on this subject? Inversely, were there any revelations you had in writing about the subject that you did not initially consider?

I had a lot of revelations about pain while writing this. Women's pain is, of course, overlooked by doctors in this country. There have been so many articles and studies about how often women's pain is dismissed—how the entire medical system is built around men's bodies to the point that doctors don't even know how to diagnose heart attacks in women. We are seen as hysterical or dramatic in our pain. Even in birth, we are made to feel guilty about easing our pain through epidurals. This was an important element to me when I was writing both "The First Time" and "American Anesthetic." This strong aversion to women getting pain relief is likely tied to fundamentalist Christianity— to Eve's consequence for eating the apple. We have been punished with pain, generations of pain above men's pain—but women who want any kind of relief, who actively seek that, are judged so much more harshly than men seeking the same thing. It's seen as a moral failing, even without the addiction aspect.

Maybe, too, this judgement is because fathers aren't expected to hold it all down the way women are—when a woman loses primary custody of her children or has Child Protective Services come knock on her door, that's so much worse than when a father abandons his family, or when he falls off the tracks, at least where I come from. Older members of my family really see men as infallible, and it's almost ancient in nature. My Mema told me early you can't expect anything of men. They're wild and perverted and unreasonable—but a woman must hold it all together. I will never forget the day my grandfather was in the hospital dying, after his self-inflicted gunshot wound. All the church men (they're Pentecostal) came to lay hands on him in his hospital bed, one of whom is a sexual predator. I was so upset to have him in the room, but to eject him would have been "disrespectful." It was my job to be quiet and polite, and even in that moment, I was encouraged to understand that and hold my tongue. Still, I'm known as the sassy, rude one, because I'm the one who won't hold my tongue, who asks why— despite all the awful things men do and have done.

Maybe this is why there aren't really poetry books about women and addiction. There are so many books and men's perspectives on the epidemic. Who gets the redemptive arc? Most shows and books are centered on men. In *Hillbilly Elegy*, the women in his life just exist to aid or foil him on his path to success. Women are taught to hold it close—to hint and cover for fear of losing everything—because we do and will lose everything. A man can be even more respected when he recovers from addiction. It shows his character, his dark past. Even looking at the difference in public perception of celebrities like Kurt Cobain and Courtney Love. There's always a clear hero and a clear villain in these stories. One is the brooding, complex man, the other is a mess. I don't believe this at all, and I think it's time we challenge those assumptions.

I have been the "cool" girl, willing to try anything once, for a lot of my life. I realized, later, I did this in part to numb myself, and for the acceptance of men. I had an idea of what it meant to be "cool" in certain crowds, so I'd never say no. This toxic way of thinking is pervasive in movies and media. It's the "broken bird" trope—a woman with trauma is "broken." A woman who can't "hang" is a prude or a bore, and one who can, well—we also see how that goes. It all comes back to the Madonna/Whore dichotomy. A man can be flawed, can fall and get redemption. Women are side characters, plot points in a man's story. I think *Dopesick* and even *Hillbilly Elegy* are great examples of this. Women's mistakes have deeper, darker consequences in both cases. A man can pull himself out. I wanted to talk about drug addiction from a woman's perspective in part to tell the story, but also because I'm so sick of that black and white vilification of women. Let women be flawed. Let mothers be flawed. Then, let them be redeemed.

Are there any pieces of media that felt integral when writing this

collection? As we mentioned above, are there any that you were actively trying to rebuke?

I don't think so, at least not while writing it. When I was writing, I was really trying to locate myself, through memories of childhood, and by going back to that place I spent so many summers. A lot of it was also in research of family documents, and of opioid addiction within the community I come from. It was the whole *write first, think about it later* aspect that I was talking about earlier. I think that helped me, in some ways. I could tell the story without worrying about speaking for anyone else. I didn't even read *Hillbilly Elegy* or watch *Dopesick* until after I had written and published many poems in *Hillbilly Madonna*.

I did think a lot about that element of who I became based on small choices, like in the movie *Sliding Doors*. Who would I be if one choice had been different? For me, I was on a very dark path. After my first year of college, I went to live with my dad who really wanted me to drop out of school and help him raise my younger siblings, who were then babies. I was at my wildest there, but something made me get up and get out. I did go back to school and, while I didn't do well at school then, it was much later that I actually got myself together, I was still saved by that in many ways.

What are you working on next? Are there any elements of Hillbilly Madonna that you want to keep exploring?

I have been working on a collection of poems based on the life of Annie Oakley, who is also an Ohio girl. There is an element of *Hillbilly Madonna* in that, though! My mother was a champion sharpshooter, and her childhood was disrupted by the shooting of her mother and grandmother by her grandfather. So, yet again, I am exploring generational trauma by researching the past. My mother has been on a journey to research her own past, and she has asked me to be a part of this, so some of the poems are based on conversations I've had with her, and questions I've asked about her childhood.

The book also explores Annie Oakley's life, and the beginnings of America, particularly how America was built on the worship of guns—and where guns have taken us as women today. I am still interested in the way gender shapes these conversations, just as with opioids. In both books, I think I am critical of the way patriarchal values have shaped this country, and how we might begin to challenge and dismantle some of those ideas.

I don't think I'll ever stop writing about these themes. This is where I come from, and these are subjects (poverty, drug use, guns, Christianity) generalized and weaponized by politicians to press and pass dangerous legislation in America today. I want to open a small door to show that there is difference and complexity everywhere.

ACKNOWLEDGEMENTS

Thank you to the following presses for first publishing these poems:

Barnhouse, "Purity Test," 2019

Birdcoat Quarterly, "Pre-Heroin," 2021

Cider Press Review, "Blood from a Turnip," 2018

EcoTheo Review, "Heroin Ghazal," 2020

The Florida Review, "Heroin as Women's Work," 2020

Fox Cry Review, "Autoimmune Anemia: Transfusion," 2014

Ghost City Review, "Old Wives Tale," 2018

Gulf Stream, "Birth Story," 2017

Harpur Palate, "Pending Charge," 2019

IDK, "I am that Farmer's Daughter" & "Sometimes the Right Light," 2016 & 2018

Illuminations, "Meleager," 2013

The Infectionist, "Girl as a Deer Shedding the Velvet," 2020

isacoustic, "A Waking Image, As Gretel," 2018

Nimrod, "Captivity Narrative," 2019

Pacific Review, "A Mark on the World," 2014

Phantom Drift, "Witch's Mark," 2018

Prism Review, "How Could She Have Known," "What My Mother Saw," & "Gross Negligence," 2020

River Mouth, "Legend Says," 2020

Rivet, "Deadbeat," 2018

Sequestrum, "Because God Demands the Silence," 2020

Slippery Elm, "On Decay," 2021 (now "Elements of Decay")

Spillway, "American Anesthetic," 2020

Tar River Poetry, "Girlhood Landscape," and "Hillbilly Madonnas," 2019 (now "Appalachia Prelude")

Third Coast, "On Cutting Him Off," 2021

The Tishman Review, "How to Cope After a Tragedy," 2018

Waxwing, "Passing It On," "Protective Services, "Narcan Metamorphosis," & "In the End, We Are All Daughters," 2020

Western Humanities Review, "This Is Where the Irritation Starts," 2019

Whale Road Review, "Mass Shooting Fallout," 2018

The Wide Shore, "I Have No Love for Images," 2016

Yellow Medicine Review, "Cattleheart," 2014

"Jack and Jill" appears in the chapbook *Tumbling After* from *Red Bird Chapbooks*

THANKS

A thousand thanks to James McNulty and Jerrod Schwarz of *Driftwood* for choosing this book, and for all their care in bringing it to life. Thanks to Cassie Mannes Murray for her help in getting it in front of as many eyes as possible. Thanks, too, to the friends and first readers who were there through every step of the shaping of this book, Kelly Moffett, Katherine Oliver, and my holiest coven of poets: Christen Noel Kauffman, Caroline Plasket, and Rae Hoffman Jager. Thanks to Rochelle Hurt for her excellent feedback. Thanks, especially, to my siblings of every sort, Dennie, Eric, Sam, Camryn, Tammy, and Courtney who grew alongside me, and who romp and roll throughout these pages. Thanks to my husband, Jon, for giving me the time, support, and encouragement to write this, and to my children, Cohen, Daisy, and Vivienne for agreeing to let me take some time for myself, in the woods or upstairs with the door closed. This book is for the sisters I have lost, for the girl I could have been, for my Mema who taught me to be fierce, and, mostly, for my mother who always kept me out of the fire, ensuring I'd grow into something better than my family history. Thanks to her, Jennifer Patton Hoang, with deep acknowledgment of the work it takes to break any cycle.

Photo by Christen Noel Kauffman

Sara Moore Wagner is the author of *Swan Wife* (winner of the 2021 *Cider Press Review* Editor's Prize), a recipient of a 2022 Individual Excellence Award from the *Ohio Arts Council*, a 2021 National Poetry Series Finalist, and the recipient of a 2019 *Sustainable Arts Foundation* award. She is the author of the chapbooks *Tumbling After* (Redbird, 2022) and *Hooked Through* (*Five Oaks Press*, 2017). Her poetry has appeared in many journals and anthologies including *Sixth Finch, Waxwing, Nimrod, Western Humanities Review, Tar River Poetry,* and *The Cincinnati Review*, among others. She lives in West Chester, OH with her filmmaker husband Jon and their children, Daisy, Vivienne, and Cohen.

MORE TITLES FROM

DRIFTWOOD PRESS

poetry, fiction, & comics

NEW!

Printed in the USA
CPSIA information can be obtained
at www.ICGtesting.com
CBHW020825180524
8578CB00003B/13